Early

Native American Recipes and Remedies

by
Duane R. Lund, Ph.D.

Based on historical research of Midwest and Canadian Indian Tribes and Alaskan and Canadian Eskimos and Aleuts.

Distributed By
Adventure Publications, Inc.
P.O. Box 269
Cambridge, MN 55008

ISBN 0-934860-57-2

TABLE OF CONTENTS

PART TWO   EARLY NATIVE AMERICAN REMEDIES

ABOUT THIS BOOK

This collection of Native American recipes and remedies is the result of many years of research, including personal interviews with the Chippewa, Sioux, Ottawa and Cree Indians of the Upper Midwest and Canada, as well as Alaskan Eskimos and Aleuts. These are original recipes and are not typical of the way these people prepare food today. However, with the addition of seasonings now available and other favorite foods, many of the recipes will provide "good eating" by today's standards.

Although some of the remedies in this book are used to this day, *none of them is recommended by the author to treat illness or disease.* They are contained in this book for purposes of historical interest and information only.

In terms of today's culture, some of the recipes and remedies may seem strange and even humorous. This book is not written, however, to entertain or to ridicule. It has often been said that necessity is the mother of invention. When faced with starvation, it is amazing how good some strange foods may taste. Before you laugh at any of the recipes, try them — you just might like them!

PART I

EARLY NATIVE AMERICAN RECIPES

CHAPTER
I
TEAS AND BEVERAGES

Most northern Indian tribes traveled a good deal, and as they traveled, they learned (probably the hard way) that the water in lakes and streams even in that day was not always safe to drink. By brewing tea, they solved that problem, and also produced a tasty beverage.

Cranberry Tea (low bush)

> 4 handfuls of cranberries - in a kettle
> 1 handful maple sugar
> Cover ingredients with water
> Boil until cranberries are soft

Use a sieve and force the juice out of the cooked mixture. (Indians made sieves out of mats woven from slender willow branches, grass or rushes.)

Sugar and/or water may be added to taste. Indians usually diluted the mixture until there was only a light cranberry flavor.

Cranberry tea was sometimes made in large quantities and was then saved and reheated as needed.

If maple sugar is not available, substitute brown sugar or table sugar.

Cranberry Tea (high bush)

High Bush cranberries aren't related to the low bush variety. You may use the same recipe, however, as for the low bush (above) but expect an entirely different flavor. Use slightly more sugar. It will taste better than it smells as you prepare it.

Rose Hip Tea

Pick the hips after the first frost when they are a bright red.
Wash and remove the "brushes".
Place in pot and cover with water.
Add a few mint leaves. (optional)
Bring to a boil, then let simmer 15 minutes.
Squash the hips, forcing out the juice.
Strain through a sieve.
Add hot water to taste.

Wintergreen Tea

Place three handfuls of wintergreen berries in a pot.
Cover with water.
Boil until berries are soft.
Mash berries.
Strain out the juice.
Add hot water to taste (about six cups of water to one cup of juice).

When berries are not in season, wintergreen leaves may be used. About a dozen leaves will make one cup of tea. Place leaves and water in pot. Bring to a boil and let simmer about 15 minutes.

Pine Needle Tea

Make a bundle of about two dozen Norway or white pine needles. New green needles in summer work best. Cut off brown ends. Bring two cups of water to a boil. Add the bundle of needles. Reduce heat and let simmer for about 15 minutes. Experiment with amounts of water and needles to suit individual taste.

Labrador Tea

The Labrador plant is found growing on muskeg or tundra. It is a small, dwarf-like plant with slender green needles (usually orangish-brown on the underside).

> Dry the leaves (in the sun or in an oven).
> Add two handfuls of dried leaves to about eight cups of boiling water.
> Reduce heat and let simmer about 10 minutes.

Catnip Tea

Add a handful of fresh leaves to a pot of boiling water (about six cups). Reduce heat and let simmer about 15 minutes.

Berry Beverages

Hot and cold drinks were made by adding the juice of almost any berries to water. Some of the more common ones were:

> blueberries
> dewberries (wild blackberries)
> raspberries
> strawberries
> chokecherries
> pincherries
> wild plums

Maple sugar was sometimes used to sweeten the drinks.

When the berries were not in season, twigs of some of these bushes were boiled in water to make tea. Favorites included chokecherries and raspberries.

> Bundle the twigs and weight them so that they will stay submerged in the water.
> Use about two ounces of twigs with four cups of water.
> Boil about 15 minutes. Remove twigs.

Berry plant leaves were also used to make tea. Fresh, young leaves work best. Rose bush leaves also make a good tea.

Flower Blossom Teas

Collect wild flower petals (such as the rose). Save just the petals — not the center of the flower. Let dry under low heat until the petals become powdery. Add about a spoonful of powdered petals to each cup of boiling water. Strain out whatever does not dissolve.

OTHER BEVERAGES

Sumac Drink

Pick the sumac fruit when it is red — late summer or fall.

    Crush the fruit in a pot.
    Cover with boiling water and allow to cool.
    Strain through a sieve.
    Add maple sugar to taste.
    Serve hot or cold.

   This drink is sometimes called "sumac lemonade".

Wild Grape Drink

Place the grapes in a kettle and cover with water.

    Mash the grapes.
    Bring to a boil and then let simmer about 15 minutes.
    Let cool.
    Strain through a sieve.
    Add maple sugar to taste (table sugar may be substituted).

Maple Sugar Drink

Add as much maple sugar to cold water as will dissolve.

CHAPTER
II
MAPLE PRODUCTS

The Indians of the Upper Midwest and Ontario cherished maple products. Sugar was preferred to syrup because it could be more easily stored and transported. When added to water it made a tasty beverage and was used as a flavoring agent for all kinds of foods. The sugar was often pressed into molds and allowed to harden and was then eaten as a candy. Special spring camps in the "sugar bush" were visited annually. Permanent lodges, called "Wig-wa-si-ga-mig" (nicknamed wigwams by the whites) were constructed from poles and recovered each year with hides and bark.

Harvesting techniques were simple but effective. A deep slice was made in the bark of the tree with a knife or tomahawk and a cedar splinter was driven into the wound to serve as a spout. The sap dripped into a birchbark container at the foot of the tree.

The sap was collected at least daily. Before the coming of the trader with his iron kettles, the Indian boiled the sap in clay vessels or by dropping very hot stones into birchbark containers filled with sap. Sugar products were made by slowly stirring the syrup in basswood troughs. Candy was made by pressing the sugar into molds and letting it harden.

Another candy treat was made by pouring the maple syrup over a container of snow.

Making syrup was a long process that required tending fires and kettles day and night. The sap had to be boiled for several days until evaporation reduced the liquid to syrup. Although the amount of sugar in the sap will

Indians made syrup by boiling sap for days over an open fire.

vary from grove to grove and even tree to tree, the final product is usually about $\frac{1}{40}^{\text{th}}$ the original quantity.

Three kettles were often used by the Indians, and the sap was ladled from one kettle to the other as it became thicker, with only the last kettle being used to make the final product.

Maple products were so important to the Indians' diet, that it was not unusual to process as much as 500 to 600 pounds of sugar per family.

A cedar spike was traditionally used as the "faucet".

CHAPTER
III
WILD RICE

Harvesting

The Upper Midwest, Manitoba, Saskatchewan and Ontario had a natural monopoly on wild rice for many years. Significant quantities are now grown in California. Wild rice was important to the Indian's diet in this part of the country and was one of the few foods that could be easily and indefinitely stored. Actually, it is not a true rice. In fact, the first French explorers described the grain in their logs as "wild oats". The commercial growers of today use artificial paddies, weed and water control, and have adapted conventional farm machinery to make possible a profitable operation. The University of Minnesota has cooperated with the farmer in developing new strains which are more resistant to wind and hail and which have non-shattering heads which means the grain may be harvested at one time, by machine, in a single operation.

The kernels of rice in the same head of the natural varieties ripen at different times over several days. This is why an area may be harvested several times over a couple of weeks' as new kernels ripen. This is also the reason the law requires the use of canoes or narrow boats so that the rice is not beaten down and wasted, but may be worked several times. There has been no improvement in the harvesting of the non-domestic rice over the method used by the Indians throughout the centuries. The stalks are simply bent over the boat and the ripe kernels are beaten from the head into the boat—usually with stout sticks.

There was also the Indian custom of tying some of the rice into bundles

The stalks are bent over the boat and the ripe
kernels are beaten from the head with a stout stick.
Courtesy Minnesota Historical Society

just before it ripened, leaving the plants to continue their growth. These were then harvested as a bundle and this rice had a different flavor and was considered a special delicacy.

Processing

As we have said, for family purposes, the Indian method has not been improved. The harvested rice was parched over or near heat, stirring slowly so that it would not burn. Once the kernels were loosened from the husks, the rice was removed from the heat and pounded. Indians used a large wooden container as a mortar and a pointed pole as a pestle. Once the separation was complete, the rice was winnowed by throwing it in the air—over a sheet of birchbark or a blanket—on a windy day. The chaff blew away. As a final step, the last remnants of husks were

The harvested rice is parched over or near heat, stirring regularly so the kernels will not burn.

removed by trampling with clean moccasins. If there were large quantities, the Indians rested their hands or elbows on poles secured to either side of a tree while trampling the rice. Once again the rice was winnowed; this time the chaff was saved and cooked like rice. The grain could be stored in a cool dry place—indefinitely.

Cooking

The wild rice was cooked in water and served as a vegetable, but it was frequently added to soups and stews and to a great variety of meat dishes. Pieces of fowl, venison and other game were often cooked with the rice, much as we prepare casseroles today.

In the case of soups and stews, the rice kernels were thrown into a kettle of water with the other ingredients and the mixture was allowed to simmer until the rice "flowered" and the meat became tender.

When used as a side dish, the rice was allowed to simmer in water for an hour or more until fully flowered out. Seasonings were usually added, such as bear fat, wild onion, ginger or maple sugar.

Other uses of wild rice in combination with other foods will be described later in this book.

Once the kernels are loosened from the husks, the rice is removed from the heat and pounded.

CHAPTER
IV
Pemmican

Although the exact origin of pemmican is unknown, the plains Indians of this part of the continent are more closely associated with the product than any other group of Native Americans. They literally manufactured tons of the commodity every year for centuries. Not only did it nourish them in travel but it sustained life itself in times of famine. White man quickly learned its value and pemmican became a major trade item by the late 1700's. Although pemmican was made from all kinds of big game animals and even fish, buffalo was the favorite and in the early 1800's Pembina, North Dakota, became the marketing center. Arctic explorers, including Perry and Byrd, used the product extensively and reported that even though their men did not relish it at first they came to find it very satisfying and even looked forward to the next meal. As late as World War I it served as a survival ration and there was even some experimentation during the Second World War.

The original Indian pemmican contained only powdered or finely chopped dried meat saturated in melted animal fat and stored in airtight animal skins. It was not uncommon to store pemmican for as long as five years. It is said that bone marrow was preferred to other fats. Few whites ever cultivated a taste for the commodity until flavor was added in the form of dried wild fruits and berries. As the trade reached its peak in the early 1800's fillers and flavoring were added, including oatmeal, potato flour, dehydrated vegetables and a variety of seasonings.

Here is a basic recipe:

Cut lean meat strips about one-half inch thick and one inch wide (any length). Indians used a variety of meat, including venison, moose, beaver, elk, buffalo, etc. (use about four pounds).

Dry the meat slowly, taking about five hours. Hang it near a fire on the side away from the smoke.* The meat is ready when it can be broken into small pieces.

Break or cut the meat strips into very small pieces.

Dry berries (such as blueberries or other seedless varieties) until they can be ground or pounded until powdery. (Use about one-half pound for four pounds of meat).

Melt an equal amount (volume) of bone marrow and/or animal fat. (See page 56 for "rendering animal fat into lard").

Stuff the powdered berries and chopped meat into cleaned animal intestines or a stomach. (You may prefer to use sausage casing.)

Pour the melted animal fat into the container, allowing it to flow through the mixture towards the bottom (by gravity).

Tie off the ends to keep air out.

Store in a cool, dry place.

Serve cold or heated. Indians often added pemmican to soups and stews.

*The meat strips may be dried in a "low" oven.

CHAPTER
V
WILDERNESS FRUITS, VEGETABLES AND OTHER PLANTS

Seasonings

Since salt was not available to many Indian tribes,* other seasonings were used, including the following:

> wild ginger,
> wild onion (tops of plants),
> sage,
> mint,
> wintergreen leaves and berries, and
> bear grease (particularly from the intestine area).

Maple sugar was used as a sweetener.

Thickening Agents

Corn silk and pumpkin blossoms were dried and powdered and then used to thicken soups, meat gravies and stews.

Cattail Sprouts

The sprouts may be harvested in early spring, shortly after the snow disappears from the marshes. The younger the sprout, the more tender the eating. (Look for them in the previous year's stand along the edges of lakes and marshes.)

> Clean and cut into one inch pieces.
> Place in a pot and cover with water.

---

*Even where salt was available, some tribes did not use it.

Add seasoning of choice (Indians originally used wild onion or ginger or maple sugar.)

Simmer over low heat until tender (just a few minutes).

The taste is similar to asparagus and may be served with the same sauces.

The spouts may also be enjoyed raw.

Cattail Bulbs (roots)

Early Native Americans ate the bulbs raw as well as cooked. Usually they would slice them before cooking or eating.

Frankly, they are not as good as the sprouts.

Cattail Fluff

The cattail heads were harvested in the fall of the year when they could easily be broken into fluff. The fluff was added to stews and soups as a thickening agent and for nutritional value.

Again, it doesn't do much for the taste.

Some modern day cooks add fluff to pancake batter (about ¼ cup fluff to one cup batter). In the author's estimation, the purpose is more conversational than flavor enhancement. If you want "really wild" pancakes, add a little cooked wild rice (about ¼ cup to one cup batter) as well as the cattail fluff.

Squash Blossoms

Early Native Americans raised squash for their meat, but they also cooked the blossoms as a vegetable. The blossoms cook very rapidly. Immerse them in boiling water for about one minute.

For a modern touch, dip the blossoms in your favorite batter (with a little seasoning, such as salt and pepper, added to the batter) and deep fat fry them in oil until brown. Pick the blossoms just before they open. The larger male blossoms work best.

Squash and Pumpkin Seeds

When roasted, the seeds take on a nutty flavor. Salt lightly before serving.

Wild Celery

Indian peoples cooked the leaves as a vegetable, but mostly they were added to other dishes as flavoring, particularly fish.

Plantain

This broad-leafed weed was cooked by the early Indians as a vegetable. It takes a little longer to cook than thinner leafed plants. Bring water to a boil and then add the leaves. Remove after three minutes.

Season and serve as greens. A little vinegar works well.

Plantain is also used for its medicinal value (page 77).

Horsetail

The young shoots in the spring of the year are best. The outer layer should be removed and discarded. What remains may be eaten raw. It has a sweet taste.

Early Indian peoples dipped the raw shoots in game drippings and then held them briefly over a fire until they were lightly smoked.

Aspen Bark

The inner bark of the aspen (poplar) tree may be eaten as is. It is rather sweet tasting. It is the sap-carrying layer.

Wood Ferns

Harvest the ferns in early spring when they still look like fiddle necks.

Clean and trim off any brown coloring.

Place several handfuls in a pot.

Cover with water.

Bring to a boil, reduce heat and let simmer about two minutes or until tender.

Seasonings used by early Indian cooks included wild ginger or a little bear fat. You may want to substitute a little salt and/or vinegar.

Greens

Greens are always best in spring when they are most tender. Varieties used by early Americans included:

dandelion

lambs quarters (Some call it "wild spinach". The tops are the most tender.)

thistle

In each case, cook them briefly with just enough water to cover them. When they "wilt", they are done. Season or sprinkle with vinegar.

(Try them with any of your spinach recipes).

Pumpkin and Squash

Both were Native American foods and found wherever Indians chose to raise gardens. Early explorers brought the seeds from these plants back to Europe.

Indian cooks used at least three methods of preparation:

Method #1:

Cut into chunks.

Leave skin on.

Scrape off seeds and "stringy" particles.

Bake by the fire, turning for even cooking.

Method #2:

    Remove the skin and the seeds.

    Cut into small pieces; place in pot.

    Add a little water and maple sugar.

    Cook over low heat until soft enough to be mashed.

Method #3:

    Cut off top (much as a child does when making a jack-o-lantern).

    Remove seeds.

    Stuff with pre-cooked wild rice.

    Add a little water to keep moist.

    Place top back on.

    Bake with low heat.

Squash and pumpkin were kept well into the winter months by storing them in pits (lined with birch bark) dug below the frostline — as deep as six feet.

Maize (corn)

Corn is native to this continent and is another food explorers brought back to Europe. Originally cultivated in warmer climates, it is believed it was brought north to the Upper Midwest by the Sioux. Indian corn required a longer growing season than today's varieties and it was difficult to raise in colder climates. For the Indians of the plains, it was the main staple food, much as wild rice was for the Woodland Indians. Corn was prepared in essentially six ways:

Method #1:

    Cut the kernels from the cob and cook with a little water and appropriate seasoning (such as sage).

Method #2:

Roasting: Remove the silk. Rewrap the husks around the ear. Soak in water until thoroughly saturated. Roast in coals until corn is cooked through by the steam.

Method #3:

Corn Bread. Let corn dry on the cob. Scrape kernels from the cob. Grind or pound (usually was done between stones) until it becomes a coarse flour. Add water gradually to make a dough. Bake on a flat rock by the fire.

Some tribes made ovens (southwest).

Sometimes a little lye water was added as the dough was made. Lye was made by boiling the ashes from hardwoods. The solution was allowed to cool. The ashes would settle out or were strained through a sieve made of willows or rushes.

Method #4:

Succotash. Corn and other vegetables (try beans) are boiled together with a little bear fat added for flavor (a sweetening effect). Use just enough water to cover.

Method #5:

Dried corn soup. Corn is allowed to dry on the cob. It is then scraped off and boiled in water. Approximately three cups of water should be used for every cup of corn. Indians used a variety of seasonings, but animal fat was often added to enhance the flavor.

Method #6:

Parched. Dried corn is scraped from the cob and cooked in a hot, covered container. It must be stirred constantly for about ten minutes.

Acorn Bread

Indians who lived too far north for corn to grow made bread from acorn flour:

> Shell dried acorns.
>
> Grind or pulverize the acorn meat into flour.
>
> Add water—including a little lye water—and make a dough.
>
> Bake on a flat rock by the fire, turning rock as needed.

As explained in the corn bread recipes above, lye water was made from hardwood ashes.

Berries

Berries of all kinds were harvested and eaten fresh from the vine, but they were also cooked, dried and added to other foods for flavor. They were also preserved for off-season use in animal fat.

Cooking

> Place cleaned berries in a pot.
>
> Add about ¼ as much maple sugar by volume as there are berries.
>
> Cover with water.
>
> Cook until the substance of a sauce.

Drying

> Dry slowly by the fire or in the sun. (It was the children's job to keep birds from helping themselves.)
>
> Dried berries and fruits were often ground into a powdery substance — seeds, pits and all.
>
> Use as a flavoring agent for other foods (wild rice, acorn bread, soups, etc.) or eat as a separate dish.

Preserved in fat

Use equal weights of deer tallow and berries.

Warm tallow until it is soft and pliable.

Work the berries into the fat.

Store in cleaned animal intestines. Keep in a cool place.

Milkweed Pods

Green (but filled out) milkweed pods were boiled in water until tender.

Try serving the cooked pods with a cheese sauce over them.

Wild Mustard

The greens were eaten raw or cooked. The stems of wild onions were chopped into short pieces and cooked or served with the greens. Indians often dripped hot, melted fat over the greens.

Wild Honey

Although northern Indians had maple sugar and candy to satisfy the "sweet tooth", honey was also treasured as a food and flavoring agent. Rarely was honey found by accident. People watched bees in flight. The insects make a "bee-line" for their hives once they are loaded with nectar and pollen. All the watchers had to do was follow the flight and look for more bees once the one they first followed was out of sight.

Nuts

Nuts of all kinds (mostly hazelnuts and filberts in the North) were peeled and dried in the shell each fall. Although added to some foods, they were usually cracked and eaten as a snack.

Winter Foods

It was critical for survival that sufficient quantities of wild rice, pemmican, maple sugar and berries be stored to go along with the game and fish taken during the winter months. (Containers of edible wild rice have been found buried at old village sites which are thought to be more than 100 years old.) About the only vegetables which could be harvested in the winter was the inner bark of such trees as the willow, aspen and birch. This was added to soups and stews for nourishment more than for flavor.

Moss and lichens were used in an emergency in the same manner. Radisson, the explorer and co-founder of the Hudson's Bay Company, compared the color, flavor and consistency of cooked lichens to glue!

CHAPTER
VI
FISH

Broiled

Method #1

Relatively small fish (less than 2#) were impaled on a green stick. The fish were not gutted. Both ends of the stick were sharpened. The smaller end was poked into the fish at the vent and run up as far as the head. The larger end was pushed into the ground alongside a camp fire. The fish could then be turned so that it was done evenly throughout.

Cooking fires were kept small, most of the heat coming from coals. Large, hot fires would not work well because the fish would end up burned on the outside and raw in the middle.

In addition to the meaty parts of the fish, the cheeks and liver were also enjoyed. If the fish had not yet spawned, the eggs or milt were also eaten – and considered a delicacy.

Method #2

Larger fish were often halved by cutting along the back bone. Each half was held by a split, green stick, pushed into the ground near a cooking fire. When one side was done, the stick was turned to expose the other side to the heat.

Method #3

Fish of any size (including panfish) were first halved by cutting along the backbone. A green stick, sharpened on both ends, was run up between the skin and the flesh – the full length of the fish. The larger end of the stick was then pushed into the ground by a fire and turned to cook both sides.

Boiled (poached)

Boiled Freshwater Herring

If the herring were netted before they spawned (and that was the prefer-ence), they were cooked whole; otherwise, they were usually gutted.

A container of water was brought to a rolling boil. If the fish had been opened and gutted, seasonings were added, such as wild onion, ginger or bear grease. (You may just want to add salt.)

When the fish were placed in the water, the boiling action would subside for a few minutes. Once the boiling resumed, it would take about 10 min-utes for the opened fish to cook and about five minutes longer if the fish were whole. When done, the backbone could be easily removed.

You may wish to pick the meat away from the bones and serve the her-ring with boiled potatoes, cream gravy, and plenty of butter.

Boiled Whitefish

The fish was first cleaned (gutted and scaled) and then cut into chunks or strips about two inches wide. You may prefer to filet the fish and remove the skin.

The fish chunks were placed in a container of cold water. Favorite sea-sonings were added. You may wish to add a few whole, black peppers, salt and a bay leaf or two. A favorite with present day Indian people is to add a chunk of salt pork.

The water was brought to a boil and then removed far enough from the coals to just simmer. When the fish flaked easily (about 10 minutes after coming to a boil), it was removed and served.

Bite-size pieces dipped in melted butter are the equal of lobster.

Baked
Baked in Clay

Whole fish, especially smaller varieties, were covered with a generous layer of clay and baked under camp fire coals. The fish were not opened or cleaned; that would have made it impossible to keep the meat dirt-free.

After the fire had burned down, the coals were raked to one side and a hole dug large enough to contain the fish. Dirt was sprinkled on top and the coals were then raked back over the hole.

After about two hours the clay would be pottery-hard and the fish baked through. The clay could be easily broken away from the fish.

If you don't like the idea of eating a fish that hasn't been gutted, try cleaning out the fish and then sealing it in foil. By covering it with clay, the fish will not burn when cooked under coals. Clay is not necessary, however, if the foil-covered fish is buried under a couple inches of dirt before being covered with coals.

Broths and Soups
Fish Soup

Chunks of fish and vegetables (Indians used wild onion shoots, corn, wild potatoes, cattail bulbs, wild rice, etc.) were placed in a container of cold water. Favorite seasonings were added, such as ginger or bear grease. (You may want to try a little salt and a sprig or two of dill.) The water was brought to a boil, and then removed far enough from the heat so that the water would just simmer. Sometimes the fish was allowed to cook away from the bones, making it easy to remove them.

Fish Stew

The above recipe for soup was followed, but powdered, dried corn silk or pumpkin flowers were added while the brew was simmering. This thickened the soup into a stew consistency. Of course, if proportionately less water was used, it was also more like a stew.

You might want to try using milk instead of water for a chowder effect. Use a double boiler so that the milk will not scorch.

Fish Head Broth

The heads were placed in a pot and covered with about an inch of water.

Indian people considered the meat in the fish heads to be especially tasty. Nearly all of the meat is in the cheeks, so these were often cut out and eaten after they had been cooked and the rest of the head was then returned to the kettle and allowed to continue simmering. Backbones of the fish were also cooked. Favorite seasonings included bear grease, wild onion, wild ginger, wild dill, etc.

After simmering until all of the flavor was extracted from the ingredients, the broth was strained and served hot.

Leftover broth was used for cooking wild rice and other vegetables.

Smoked Fish Soup

This is an Eskimo dish, but once Indians began smoking fish they also cooked variations of this recipe.

Smoked, deboned fish are broken into bite-size pieces. Water is added (the amount depending on how thick one wants the soup). The fish and greens or vegetables are added just after the water comes to a boil. The heat is then reduced so the soup will just simmer (about 15 minutes).

Appropriate seasonings may be added, such as dill, wild celery, onion tops, etc.

Roe and Milt

Method #1 - raw

Roe and milt were either mixed or eaten separately without cooking. Whitefish seemed to be the favorite.

Usually, the eggs and/or milt was thoroughly cooled or chilled before eating. Carefully remove the blue vein from the milt.

If you would like to try it raw, try adding salt, pepper and chopped onion and chilling the mixtures in the refrigerator for 24 hours.

Method #2 - broiled or fried

All kinds of fish eggs were enjoyed. Sometimes they were broiled on racks made of green sticks or on a flat rock by the fire. When iron cooking utensils became available, the eggs were fried in grease (animal fat).

Maple sugar was sometimes sprinkled on just before serving.

You might enjoy crappie or sunfish eggs dipped in batter and fried along with your fish.

Method #3 - boiled

Both eggs and milt were cooked in water. Because they are quite delicate, care was taken to not let the water come to a rolling boil. The milt is especially fragile and has a blue vein which should be removed before cooking.

Seasonings were usually added; you might try adding a little lemon juice to the water.

Method #4 - fish intestines and fish eggs

The intestines of large fish were removed, reversed, and washed thoroughly. They were then chopped into small pieces and fried with the roe. Milt was sometimes added.

Fish Liver

The livers of larger fish, such as the northern pike and eelpout were seldom wasted.

They were enjoyed baked, broiled or fried.

Expect fish liver to taste like animal liver, only milder.

Preserving Fish

Freezing

Fish caught in winter were frozen whole and covered by an ice glaze to seal in the moisture. This was accomplished by dipping the frozen fish in the ice water at least twice for a good coat.

Drying

Fish were usually dried slowly by the fire on the side away from the smoke. They were turned for even drying on both sides.

In the summer when it was very hot and dry (low humidity), fish were hung on racks and dried in the sun. The farther north, the less the humidity.

Most fish (all but the smallest — such as perch) were split lengthwise and opened so that they could dry more quickly and thoroughly. With larger fish, the head was left on and the fillets cut away from both sides of the backbone. They were left attached to the head by the skin. The fish were then hung over racks with the backbone and tail on the one side and the fillets on the other.

Panfish were dried by laying the halves on a network of green branches.

Before eating, the dried fish were usually cut up and boiled.

Partial Drying plus Maple Sugar

When the fish had been partly dried, the meat was removed from the bones. It was then spread on a clean surface, such as birchbark, and worked by hand until it became a smooth, fine texture—like putty. Maple sugar was then worked into the mixture and it was stored in birchbark containers.

Smoking

Preservation by smoking came in more modern times and was (and still is) done in "smoke houses" where the smoke may be concentrated. Heat is kept quite low.

CHAPTER
VII
OTHER WATER CREATURES

Freshwater Lobster

Freshwater crawfish are the small cousins of the huge, saltwater lobsters. Early Americans prepared them in the same manner, however:

> Bring a container of water to a boil.
>
> Drop in the live crawfish.
>
> When they turn red (it only takes a few minutes), they are ready to be peeled. The claws are too small to bother with. The tail piece, however, is bite-size and delicious when dipped into salted, melted butter.

Freshwater Clams

Freshwater clams are relatively scarce today. When early white settlers arrived in the late 19th and early 20th centuries, huge quantities were harvested for their shells. Special factories were built for processing them into pearl buttons and jewelry.

To be eaten, they may be opened with a heavy knife or other sharp instrument. The muscle should be cut away from the shell. The neck and jelly-like substance should be discarded.

Clams may be boiled, broiled, or fried.

Indian people usually added the clams to fish soups and stews.

Frogs

Indians rarely bothered with small frogs (the kind we use for fish bait) but the larger varieties—usually called "bull frogs"—were cherished for their hind legs. To process them:

> Cut the hind legs off at the hip.
>
> Cut off the feet.
>
> Peel off the skin as you would a glove.
>
> They may be fried or broiled.

Snapping Turtles

Butchering

Both the claws and the head are "lethal", and should be removed before operating. Begin by chopping off the head. Let the turtle hang, head down for a couple of hours because the nervous system will react at least that long after the head is removed. The "dying" process can be speeded up by boiling the turtle for a half hour; this will also make it easier to clean. Now chop off the claws. The first few times you try it the turtle will be easier to handle if you lay him on his back on a board or old table and drive a nail through each "claw".

The next step is to remove the bottom shell. Locate the soft cartilage "crack" where the upper and lower shells are joined on each side; this may be cut with a knife. Cut away any skin that holds the lower shell. After removing the lower shell, skin the legs and remove them — including the thighs. Next, remove the meat around the neck and at the base of the shell (tail end). You will have now salvaged about 90% of the meat, so the remainder may be discarded.

Soups and Stews

Because turtle meat is often tough, Indians usually cooked it as a base for soups and stews. The meat was cut into bite-size pieces, covered in a pot with water, and allowed to simmer for an hour or so until tender.

Vegetables and/or wild rice were cooked with the meat.

You may want to use beef broth instead of water.

Broiled

Indians probably broiled turtle meat over the coals, but it was no doubt pretty chewy.

Baked (modern Indian recipe, Cass Lake, Mn.)

Disjoint and/or cut into serving size pieces.

Roll in seasoned flour and brown in oil.

Place meat in baking dish and cover with cream of mushroom soup or tomato sauce. Place in slow oven for two hours or until tender.

Fried (modern day recipe)

Marinate (refrigerated) for 24 hours in the following sauce:

½ cup salad oil

2 tablespoons soy sauce

¼ cup sugar

¼ cup finely chopped onion

½ teaspoon salt

½ teaspoon pepper

4 teaspoons sesame seed

CHAPTER
VIII
BIG GAME

For early Native Americans, big game was the major source of meat. This included deer, bear, buffalo, elk, caribou, and moose. Although elk are now in the west and caribou in the far north, both were in Minnesota and Wisconsin before 1900. There were years when these large animals became scarce for one reason or another, and people were forced to survive on rabbits and other small animals.

Very little of the big game animal was wasted — particularly during difficult times. In addition to steaks, chops, and roasts, other edible parts included the heart, kidneys, brains, liver, intestines, tripe, head meat and tongue. The bone marrow was nearly always eaten, and was considered a delicacy. In fact, a specially carved stick for taking out the cooked marrow was a utensil used by every member of the family.

The stomach and intestines were often reversed and washed, and then used to store foods. The small intestines of some animals were cleaned and then chopped into short pieces and fried.

The hides were used for clothing and as covering for the lodges. Strips of hide were made into thongs and woven into snowshoes. They also served as bow strings, although the very best bow strings were made from turtle sinew. When hides were used for clothing or as bedding, they were made soft by endless hours of chewing.

Broiled

Before pots and pans were available, most meat was broiled over coals —

probably on a spit. Because of the convenience and the excellent flavor imparted by this method, broiling has continued to be a favorite way of cooking meat right up to the present.

Although steaks could be broiled in a matter of minutes, up to a full day was required to roast a hind quarter. Older children were given the responsibility for rotating the meat so that it cooked evenly.

Roasting in Pots

When iron kettles became available from the fur traders, they were suspended over coals and used for cooking a great variety of things, including roasts. A little water or animal fat was placed in the bottom to prevent burning.

Vegetables, such as wild potatoes, onions, Jerusalem artichoke, cow-parsnip roots, corn or wild rice, were frequently added — not unlike our New England boiled dinners.

Soups and Stews

Tougher cuts of meat were cut into small pieces and made more tender by stewing them in water. The liquid was sometimes given a gravy-like consistency by adding dried, powdered corn silk or pumpkin blossoms.

Vegetables were frequently added, just as we do today.

Bones (sometimes with scraps of meat attached) left over from roasting were used as a base for soup or broth.

Wild Rice Stew (present day Indian recipe, Lake of the Woods)

> 1 cup wild rice
> 2 pounds stew meat
> 1 onion, chopped
> 1 cup celery, chopped
> 1 can cream of mushroom soup

½ cup green pepper, chopped
⅛ pound butter
1 can mushrooms (4 oz.)

Prepare the wild rice by simmering in water until kernels flower out.

Cut meat into bite-size pieces. Brown in a hot skillet.

Sauté onion, celery and green pepper in butter over low heat until onions are clear (three or four minutes).

Use a greased, covered baking dish. Place all ingredients in the baking dish and mix well. Cover and bake two hours in medium oven (350°).

Add water if necessary to prevent dryness.

Tongue

The tongue was boiled (for about an hour) in water seasoned with bear grease, or wild ginger or dill, or some combination thereof.

The root ends were then cut off and the skin split and peeled off. The tongue was sliced and served.

Pickled Tongue (a present day Indian recipe)

For four to six deer tongues:

1 pt. vinegar
1 pt. water
2 tablespoons sugar
1 teaspoon whole cloves
1 teaspoon whole allspice
1 teaspoon whole black peppers
½ teaspoon mustard seed
½ teaspoon salt

Wash tongues in salted water. Place in fresh water. Add one tablespoon allspice, and let simmer one to two hours or until tender. (It will never get really tender.) Let cool and peel off skin and cut off root ends. Place in jars and submerge in a pickling solution prepared from the above ingredients which has been boiled for about 10 minutes.

Refrigerate and let stand one week before eating.

Heart

The heart from any big game animal was a favorite of early Native Americans. It was broiled whole, sliced and fried, or cut into chunks and added to stews or soups.

Here's a modern day Indian recipe (from Mille Lacs Lake) for stuffed heart you may like to try:

Clean the heart, cut open and remove arteries, veins and fat. Prepare stuffing of two cups of dried bread pieces, ¼ cup chopped celery, ¼ cup chopped onion, and seasoned to taste with salt and pepper. Add generous pats of butter as you stir the mixture together.

Stuff heart and close opening with skewers. Season outside of heart with salt and pepper. Roll in flour, and brown in cooking oil. Bake in medium oven (325°) for 1½ hours. Slice and serve with stuffing. (Extra stuffing may be baked in foil alongside the heart.)

Jellied Moose Nose (present day seasonings added)

The nose of the moose has long been considered a delicacy by Native Americans. Early white settlers also enjoyed it—usually roasted.

Use the nose, cutting off the upper jaw bone just under the eyes. Boil in a large kettle for 45 minutes. Cool. Now the hair may be easily removed.

Submerge the nose in fresh water. Add a chopped onion, two tablespoons pickling spices and one bay leaf. Let simmer until tender.

Cool overnight in the same liquid.

Remove the bone and cartilage. You will find the bulb of the nose contains white meat. The thin strips along the bones and jowls will be dark. Slice both the light and dark meat, thin. Pack in jars and cover with the liquid in which the nose was boiled.

The liquid will jell when kept in a cool place.

Serve cold.

Brains

Brains of big game animals were seldom wasted; they were relished by most tribes.

After washing and removing loose membranes, the brains were simmered in seasoned water for 30 minutes. They were then fried in hot fat.

Brains may also be sautéed in butter or margarine. Season with a little salt and pepper. Dip in light pancake or corn meal batter. Stir gently as they cook. It takes about ten minutes.

Kidneys

Skin, tubes and loose membranes were removed. The kidneys were then simmered in water for about 30 minutes. This water was poured off and fresh water added (enough to cover the kidneys). Favorite seasonings such as wild onion shoots, bear grease or ginger were added and the simmering continued for another 30 minutes.

The kidneys were sliced and served hot. They were also cut into chunks and added to stews.

Liver

Liver was customarily sliced and fried in animal fat; it was seldom added to other dishes.

Rendering Animal Fat into Lard

Fat was rendered just as soon as convenient after the animal was killed. The back fat of most animals was preferred. The stomach fat of bear was used for seasoning.

All the lean meat was cut away and the fat cut into small cubes (one inch). The fat was then melted in a kettle over a hot fire. Care was taken, however, not to let the lard smoke. It was stirred frequently with a wooden paddle. When the cracklings became yellow and no more moisture was seen rising from the lard, the kettle was removed from the fire and the liquid drawn off into another container and cooled.

When it took on a creamy texture, it was stirred vigorously and then kept in a cool place.

The journals of early traders and explorers tell of trading with the Indians for lard.

CHAPTER
IX
SMALL GAME ANIMALS

Early Native Americans ate almost every kind of mammal—except the marten. Why not the marten? Research has not revealed the answer, and the author hasn't had the courage to find out for himself! Just because early Americans ate almost every other kind of animal does not mean that all were enjoyed. It's just that when food was in short supply any nourishment was welcome—and that is true even today in many parts of the world. But it is true that animals were trapped not only for their pelts but also for their meat.

Beaver

The beaver is an example of an animal that was not only a favorite for its fur but was also a favorite to eat. It was considered a delicacy and was often reserved for special feasts and occasions. White explorers and traders were frequently honored with a meal featuring roast beaver. Zebulon Pike, for example, when exploring the upper Mississippi, reported that he was welcomed by French traders on Leech Lake with a beaver banquet.

Roast Beaver

The animal was skinned, dressed and all fat removed. Particular care was taken to remove the scent glands, not only because they would adversely effect the flavor, but because they were dried and the shavings were used as a lure for trapping all kinds of animals. The tail was cut off, skinned and prepared separately.

In early years, the carcass was prepared over coals on a spit. Care was taken to pierce the body in such a way that the weight was balanced so that as the meat was rotated it stayed in position.

In later years, the beaver was disjointed and cooked in kettles. Leftovers were added to soups and stews.

Beaver Tail

The tail was prepared in at least three ways—but first it had to be skinned. This was accomplished by making a cut the full length of the tail (usually the under-side), and then peeling the skin away from the meat with the help of a knife.

Method #1:

The tails of young beaver were left whole and broiled over coals.

Method #2:

The tails of young beaver were sliced into cross-section steaks and fried in fat.

Method #3:

The tails of larger (older) beaver were tougher and were cut into bite-size pieces and added to stews and soups.

An Ontario trapper suggested this up-dated recipe:

Skin the tail of a small or medium size beaver (under 25#).

Slice into ½ inch steaks and marinate overnight in a solution of:

½ cup vinegar

1 T salt

enough water to cover the tail

(refrigerate)

Season steaks with salt and pepper, roll in flour, and brown in cooking oil.

Once the meat has been browned, add the following to the skillet:

> ½ cup red cooking wine
>
> 1 - 4 oz. can mushroom pieces
>
> 1 medium onion, chopped
>
> enough water to cover the meat

Let simmer (covered) about 45 minutes or until tender.

Garnish with mushrooms and serve.

Raccoon

After the animal was skinned and dressed, all fat was removed, as well as the bean-shaped glands under each leg.

The carcass was then broiled over coals on a spit.

If you try this, allow four or five hours for cooking—depending on the size of the animal. You may also wish to baste with your favorite barbecue sauce two or three times during the last hour of roasting.

An alternative is to stuff a small raccoon with your favorite dressing and roast (in a roaster) in a medium oven (325°) until tender (about three hours).

Muskrat

Early Native Americans fried muskrat pieces much as we fry chicken. Care was taken, however, to remove all fat from the skinned, cleaned animal.

If you wish to try muskrat, cut it into four quarters. Wipe the meat with a solution of vinegar and water (1 to 3) and marinate in salt water for 12 hours (refrigerate).

Roll quarters in seasoned flour* (salt and pepper added) and brown in oil. Add one medium, chopped onion to the pan during the frying process.

*Instead of flour, you may prefer your favorite chicken batter or cracker crumbs.

Porcupine

Porcupines are not particularly tasty and their hide is worthless (although quills were used for decorating clothing) but they were often used as a source of food by early Native Americans because they were so easy to kill.

Most of the meat is on the legs and these were either broiled or fried.

If porcupine interests you, a little "doctoring" will help:

> Cut away the four quarters from the carcass and trim off all fat. Soak in salted water, to which two tablespoons of vinegar has been added, for 12 hours.
>
> Drain and pat dry. Season lightly with salt and pepper and dredge in flour. Brown in oil. (Use bacon grease if available).
>
> Place porcupine quarters in an iron kettle. Cover with onion slices. Meanwhile, make a gravy in the skillet in which you browned the meat. Do this by pouring off excessive grease—leaving about three tablespoons of drippings in the pan. Stir in a mixture of flour and water. Continue stirring over low heat until the "right" consistency. Pour gravy over meat in the kettle, cover and let simmer on top of stove or in a low oven for two hours or until tender, occasionally basting the meat with the gravy.
>
> If you enjoy mushrooms, add some during the simmering process.

Fried porcupine liver is considered to be quite tasty.

Rabbits and Squirrels

Indian children usually snared these smaller animals or shot them with their blunted wooden arrows. Often this was the first game they brought home. Both animals were mainstays of the early Americans' diet.

Originally, rabbits and squirrels were broiled over coals—whole. With the coming of iron kettles, they were often cut into smaller pieces and fried in fat, much as we do today. On other occasions, the meat was stripped from the bone and added to stews or soups.

Here are a couple of modern day recipes you might like:

Baked Squirrel

> 4 squirrels, dressed but left whole
>
> 2 large onions, quartered
>
> 1 large onion, sliced
>
> 4 slices bacon—the fatter the better
>
> salt and pepper inside and out

Place in baking dish, side by side, back sides up on top of the quartered onions. In other words, stuff the body cavities with onion as best you can. Cut bacon slices in two and place on backs of squirrels alternately with onion slices. Cover and bake in 350° oven between 1-1/2 and 2 hours or until tender.

Old Country Rabbit Recipe

> 2 snowshoe or cottontail rabbits
>
> ½ cup cooking oil
>
> 1 cup cooking wine
>
> 2 onions, sliced
>
> 1 tablespoon allspice
>
> 1 teaspoon salt, a couple of dashes of pepper
>
> ¼ cup flour
>
> 2 tablespoons sugar

Cut the rabbits into pieces as you would a chicken. Make a marinade of the oil, wine, onions, allspice, salt and pepper. Cover meat; cover dish; refrigerate and marinate for two days. Drain on paper towel, but save marinade.

Dredge meat in seasoned flour and brown in cooking oil. Remove rabbit and pour off all oil and fats. Return meat to pan and cover with marinade, adding sugar. Bring to a boil, then reduce heat and simmer until tender (about 45 min. to 1 hour).

Rattlesnake

The plains Indians considered rattlesnake very good eating. The snake was skinned and drawn (gutted), cut into cross-sections and fried in animal fat or broiled over coals.

Skunk

Skunk does not taste like it smells! In fact, the meat is light-colored and usually tender.

Small skunks were cut up and fried; larger ones were roasted

If you decide to "tackle" one, skin and clean thoroughly, removing all fat and scent glands. Marinate 24 hours in a solution of salt water and vinegar (2 T). Refrigerate. Pat dry before frying or roasting.

Otter

Otter was also a favorite of the early Indians.

Any of the beaver recipes work well. For a variation, try making shish-ka-bobs of bite-size chunks of otter that have first been marinated overnight.

Broil over coals.

CHAPTER
X
BIRDS AND EGGS

Early Native Americans ate almost any birds' eggs large enough to make the effort to harvest and cook them worthwhile. Although grouse, seagull and duck eggs were preferred, none were spared during times of hunger—not even the loon or the robin. This was also true of the birds themselves. Passenger pigeons—now extinct—were once so common that migrations "darkened the skies". Both the bird and its eggs were Indian favorites. With the coming of whiteman and the shotgun, the pigeons were literally shot off, the last survivors being reported early in this century.

Broiled Birds

Birds, regardless of size, were most often plucked, dressed and barbecued over coals on a spit. The preparation was fast and simple and the flavor at its best.

In a Kettle

Tougher birds, such as mergansers and ducks that appeared to be older, were stewed in a pot of water. Although sometimes skinned, they were usually plucked, dressed and cooked whole.

In the Upper Midwest and Central Canadian provinces, wild rice was often added to the pot and cooked with the fowl. When the meat was tender enough to be easily picked from the bones, the meal was declared "ready".

Soups and Stews

Leftover meat was often added to soups and stews. The picked-over carcasses were frequently used as a base for making soup or broth.

Eggs

In spring and early summer, children delighted in harvesting birds' eggs for family use. Of course, the larger birds laid the more desirable eggs, such as ducks, geese, grouse, seagulls, etc.

It mattered little what state of development the embryo happened to be in. The eggs were cooked in boiling water and enjoyed.

Early voyageur cooks often added wild birds' eggs to their preparations.

Modern Game Bird Recipes
From Leech Lake, Minnesota

Mushroom Casserole

Dissect the bird as for frying.

Salt and pepper each piece.

Roll in flour.

Brown each piece in cooking oil or margarine over medium heat.

Place in a casserole or baking dish and cover with mushroom soup. (Add one can of water for each can of soup.) If you are a mushroom fancier, add a can of parts and pieces.

Place in preheated 300° oven for an hour and a half.

Your wild birds will never be dry or tough.

Wild Rice and Partridge or Duck Casserole

1 cup wild rice (washed)

flour

1 partridge, duck or pheasant—deboned and cut up into pieces

1 large onion, chopped

1 green pepper, chopped

1 small jar pimentos

1 can mushroom soup
1 can water
salt and pepper

Prepare the wild rice by letting it simmer in 2 quarts of water until "flowered" (about one hour).

Cut the bird into bite-size pieces, removing all bones. Season, roll in flour and fry in oil slowly over low heat until browned but not "crusty". When it is about done, add the chopped onion, green pepper and celery. Continue frying for another three or four minutes. Add pimento, soup and water.

Place in a greased casserole. Cover and bake in a 300° oven for 1½ hours. Add water while baking to prevent dryness.

If duck is used, cook it first in a crock-pot or very slow oven until the meat can be easily stripped away from the bones.

CHAPTER
XI
ESKIMO RECIPES

Eskimos and Aleuts enjoyed many of the same foods prepared in the same ways as we have described for the Indian peoples of the Upper Midwest and central Canada. They did have their specialties, however, some of which we will share here.

Duck not Yet

This Eskimo delicacy calls for harvesting duck eggs just prior to their being hatched. The eggs are then hard-boiled. The unhatched baby birds are unbelievably tender and succulent.

Fermented Salmon Eggs and Heads

When the salmon spawning run is over, the fish are preserved by smoking or drying. The heads and eggs are enjoyed in several ways, but one favorite for some Eskimos is to fill an empty 55 gallon oil or gasoline drum with alternate layers of salmon eggs and heads. They are allowed to ferment for a couple of weeks and then eaten as is, without further preparation.

Salmon Eggs

Salmon eggs may be fried, broiled or poached. Eskimo children enjoy them dried in the sun. Discarded jar covers are often used for this purpose. The eggs are dried in a single layer. Salt is sometimes added.

Jerky

Because of the low humidity in Alaska and northern Canada, meat (such as moose or caribou) can be cured into jerky by simply cutting the meat into narrow strips and then hanging them in the sun to dry for several days. The meat may also be dried by a fire or in a low oven (150°) for five or six hours.

Squaw Candy

Squaw candy is made of strips of salmon dried in the sun until they are delightfully chewy. The process takes three or four days. (In more humid climates, use an oven).

Whole Duck in a Fire

Hungry hunters away from home sometimes don't bother to clean ducks, but make a fire, thoroughly wet the feathers, and then lay the bird in the flames. By the time the feathers are burned off, the duck is cooked. The bird is then cleaned and eaten.

Tongue

Many Eskimos consider the tongue to be the most delicious part of any big game animal.

Preparation is simple. Tongues are simmered in water for one to two hours or until the meat is relatively tender. (Tongue never gets really tender). The size of the tongue determines the cooking time; one hour for a moose or caribou calf, two hours for an adult animal.

After cooking, the skin of the tongue is peeled off and the root ends cut off. The tongue is then sliced and served. It makes excellent sandwich meat.

Here is an Iliamna Eskimo's recipe for pickled tongue:

For four to six caribou tongues:

      1 pt. vinegar
      1 pt. water
      2 tablespoons sugar

1 teaspoon whole cloves
1 teaspoon whole allspice
1 teaspoon whole black peppers
½ teaspoon mustard seed
½ teaspoon salt

Wash tongues in salted water. Place in fresh water. Add 1 tablespoon allspice, and let simmer one to two hours or until relatively tender. Let cook and peel off skin and cut off root ends. Place in jars and submerge in a pickling solution prepared from the above ingredients which has been boiled for about 10 minutes.

Refrigerate and let stand one week before eating.

Duck Soup

This technique comes from the Alaskan Peninsula:

A cleaned duck is hung in the smoke house, head down.

The body cavity is made to hold liquid by twisting a wire around the neck skin. A can of soup of your choice (vegetable works well) is poured into the duck.

The duck is then smoked until done (about 8-10 hours). The soup keeps the meat moist and adds flavor as well.

The author can guarantee that you will enjoy the duck, he cannot guarantee that you will enjoy the soup!

Broiled Caribou Heads

The head of the caribou is severed from the body at the place where the neck joins the head. Antlers are removed and the head is skinned. The whole head is then suspended over coals and barbecued until done. This takes most of a day. Nearly everything is eaten: brains, eyes, cheek cutlets, etc.

Vegetables

Eskimos make use of plants indigenous to their area in much the same way as the Indians farther south. Because of the short growing season in the Arctic, the opportunities are more limited. Fireweed shoots, cattail shoots and bulbs, bull rush bulbs and thistle leaves are some examples.

Berries

There are more berries per acre and more varieties of berries in the Arctic than farther south. A few examples are cranberries, blueberries, lingenberries, mossberries, blackberries, bunchberries and salmonberries.

Eskimos use them in much the say way as described in the earlier chapters.

There is one notable exception:

Eskimo Ice Cream (Aguduk)

Although most any berry may be used, blueberries are the favorite.

About one-third cup of seal oil (you may use solid Crisco or other shortening) is beaten until the white fluff fills a large bowl. One cup of sugar and four cups of berries are then added. The whole mixture is gently stirred (by hand) until all that remains are sugar-coated berries. The reason it is called "ice cream" is that the berries are usually chilled before they are eaten.

Fireweed

The name comes from the fact that it springs up after a fire. It is especially plentiful in Alaska and northern Canada. Eskimos and Indians cut the young sprouts into sections and boil them until tender.

Russian Reunion*

This recipe is a leftover from the days when Alaska was owned by Russia.

---

*Courtesy Mrs. Irene Carlson, Lake Clark, Alaska

1# smoked salmon (preferably canned; smoked salmon — use 1 quart.)
2 cans tomatoes
2 large onions, cubed

Cut the salmon into bite-size pieces. Place all ingredients in a pot and simmer 40 minutes.

Serve with boiled potatoes.

Broiling Caribou heads and beaver carcasses at an Inuit potlatch.
Courtesy of Jim Lavrakas, "Alaska" magazine

PART II

EARLY NATIVE AMERICAN RECIPES

EARLY NATIVE AMERICAN REMEDIES

Medicine is not a new art; it has been practiced as long as humans have sought relief from their ailments. Early Native American practitioners prescribed medicines, applied healing balms, and even performed surgery (in that they amputated infected limbs). They administered enemas with the help of an animal bladder and a hollow straw or reed. Sometimes the healing was through faith in the Great Spirit, in the medicine man's treatments, or even in magic charms.

Although most of these early physicians were indeed medicine *men*, women were also practitioners—particularly in the art of collecting and preserving herbs and other plants. Some women became so respected and well known that people traveled hundreds of miles for their medicines. An elderly Salteaux Indian in Northern Saskatchewan told of an "old woman" who practiced medicine in his village when he was a young man, he said that she had developed her own version of "the pill" to prevent pregnancies. "She also had medicine for helping women have babies," he added.

Even today Native American practitioners are sometimes credited with success where university trained physicians may fail. A Northwest Territory native boasted, "I have never known an Indian in our village to die from cancer if he followed the instructions of our medicine man."

He insisted native practitioners had cures for cancer. When pressed for the reason these secrets were not shared with the rest of the world, he replied, "Whiteman would only use it to make money."

Nevertheless, please remember that the remedies on the following pages are *not recommended by the author*. They have been collected and are reported only for their historical interest.

Preparation of Medicines

Although parts of some plants were used "green", in most cases the leaves or roots were dried and ground into powder. The drying process was aided by hanging the plants (usually upside down) over or near a fire. A Lake of the Woods (Ontario) Indian told of visiting his grandmother's summer lodge and seeing plants hanging from the ceiling. The dried leaves or roots were usually carefully crushed into powder in the palm of the hand, using the thumb as a pestle. The powders were then kept in leather pouches or birch bark containers (indefinitely). Each was marked in code for easy identification.

Sometimes roots, stems and/or leaves were burned or charred and the ash used as a pharmaceutical ingredient.

Medications were not limited to plants and herbs; a Mille Lacs Lake (Minnesota) Indian told of "the old folks" grinding clam shells into a powder. He recalled that they were first burned in a fire to make the powdering process easier.

Bear grease, goose and duck fat, and deer tallow were used as ointments and as a medium for other medicines.

CHAPTER
XII
AILMENTS AND THEIR REMEDIES

Headache
1. Chewing on the stems of aspen leaves.
2. Chewing the inner bark of the yellow willow.
3. Blood letting. Gashes were cut—with a sharp device—in the temple area. Leeches were sometimes attached to the temple.
4. A tea was made from the flowers and leaves of the cowslip.

External Infection
Several large, wetted plantain leaves were laid over the infected wound and tied in place. The leaves were kept wet and held in place at least one day or until the infection cleared up.

Snake or Poisonous Insect Bites
The bite or fang marks were cut open to facilitate bleeding. Blood was even sucked from the wound and spit out. Plantain leaves (wetted) were applied and tied in place. The plantain leaves were credited with the power to draw the poison from the wound.

External Ulcer
A poultice, made of powdered clam shells worked into bear grease, was applied.

Swelling from Sprain or Injury
Anything cold was applied (ice, if available). If swelling continued, blood-letting from the affected area was achieved by cutting several deep gashes

with flint or with a knife. Bruised (black and blue areas) were similarly drained.

Leeches were sometimes allowed to attach themselves to the affected areas.

Constipation

1. An enema was administered, using an animal bladder (such as from a deer) and a hollow reed (as from a horsetail or bull rush). The solution injected was prepared by boiling a handful of inner birch bark shavings in about two cupfuls of water for about 20 minutes. The bark was then strained out and the liquid allowed to cool before putting it into the bladder. Because the hole in the bladder was so small, it was easier to submerge the bladder in the liquid and fill it that way. The hollow reed was then tied in place—with nettle fiber or spruce roots—and the enema administered.

2. Drink several cups of hot water or tea.

External Bleeding

1. Bear grease (or other grease) was generously applied to the wound.

2. Goose or duck down was mixed with powdered pursh root. Enough water was added to form a salve so that it would stay in place. Lard was also used as a binding agent.

Coughing

1. Powdered ginseng root and/or root of bloodroot were dissolved in water and gargled.

2. A cough syrup was made from heated pine tar.

3. Wild onion juice flavored with honey or maple sugar.

4. Honey.

5. Tea made from inner aspen bark.

Colds and Sore Throats
1. Skunk fat was rubbed on the throat and chest areas.
2. Goose grease was used similarly.

Rheumatism
1. Bear gall was rubbed on affected areas.
2. Sweat lodge treatment.

Frostbite
Rubbed with snow. The rubbing was continued after the snow had melted. (This is really not a good idea; tissue may be damaged. Rubbing with warm water is less hazardous.)

Stomachache
1. Hot broth.
2. Chokecherry bark was simmered in water and drunk as a tea.

Fever
Powdered roots of the bluebell (flower) were dissolved in water and drunk cold.

Burns
A poultice was applied, using liquid derived from simmering slippery elm bark in water.

Diarrhea
1. Crushed blackberry roots, steeped in water. Drunk as a hot tea.
2. A syrup was made from equal parts of dandelion root, blackcherry and ash bark.

Bee and Other Insect Stings
Mud was applied—the blacker the better.

Dangerously Infected Limbs (life threatening)
Amputation.

Open Wounds that do not Heal
A very hot piece of metal or stone was used to "burn out" the infected area.

Earache
Hot packs were applied; dry heat was preferred.

Fever
Cold packs and rest.

Indigestion
1. Mint leaf tea.
2. A cold bath.
3. Drink cold water—but not "too much".
4. Rose hip tea.

Foot Problems
Soak feet in as hot water as one can stand.

Piles (hemorrhoids)
Tea made from slippery elm bark.

Boils
Rub with juice squeezed from the tops of the wild onion.

Breathing Disorders

1. Honey.
2. Tea made from the stem and roots of burdock.

Poison Ivy, Sumac or Oak

Pieces of alder bark were covered with water and boiled until "syrupy"; the liquid was then applied to the affected area.

The Sweat Lodge

This Indian and Eskimo version of the Finnish sauna was used for a variety of ailments, including colds, sore muscles, rheumatism, pneumonia, and general aches and pains. Medications were sometimes added to the water used to splash on hot rocks to make the steam. Flowers were sometimes added for their perfume and also to aid breathing.

It was customary for weary hunters or warriors to seek rejuvenation in the sweat lodge.

Inhaling Vapors

Powdered herbs were sprinkled on hot stones and the vapors inhaled. The patient often covered him/herself with a blanket to concentrate the vapors.

Combinations of wild dried flowers sprinkled on hot rocks were said to aid breathing difficulties.

Although some of the remedies in this book are used to this day, none of them is recommended by the author to treat illness or disease. They are contained in this book for purposes of historical interest and information only.

Other Books by Duane R. Lund
Andrew, Youngest Lumberjack
A Beginner's Guide to Hunting and Trapping
A Kid's Guide to Fishing Secrets
Fishing and Hunting Stories from The Lake of the Woods
Lake of the Woods, Yesterday and Today, Vol. 1
Lake of the Woods, Earliest Accounts, Vol. 2
Our Historic Boundary Waters
Our Historic Upper Mississippi
The North Shore of Lake Superior, Yesterday and Today
Tales of Four Lakes and a River
The Youngest Voyageur
White Indian Boy
Nature's Bounty for Your Table
101 Favorite Freshwater Fish Recipes
101 Favorite Wild Rice Recipes
101 Favorite Mushroom Recipes
Camp Cooking, Made Easy and Fun
Sauces, Seasonings and Marinades
The Scandinavian Cookbook
Gourmet Freshwater Fish Recipes Quick and Easy
101 Ways to Add to Your Income
The Indian Wars

About the Author

- EDUCATOR (RETIRED, SUPERINTENDENT OF SCHOOLS, STAPLES, MINNESOTA);

- HISTORIAN (PAST MEMBER OF EXECUTIVE BOARD, MINNESOTA HISTORICAL SOCIETY);
  Past Member of BWCA and National Wilderness Trails Advisory Committees;

- TACKLE MANUFACTURER (PRESIDENT, LUND TACKLE CO.);

- WILDLIFE ARTIST, OUTDOORSMAN.